I am a ~~~~

A POSITIVE AFFIRMATION BOOK

BY: THE ASTROLOGY MAMA

A Letter from the Author to the Parents:

Astrology has become such a useful tool in my life and I'm happy to share a collection of zodiac inspired positive affirmation books. I believe astrology combined with positive affirmations can be a springboard into self-discovery and building self-esteem and confidence for the old and young alike.

Some of the words may be challenging depending on your child's reading level but they can provide a wonderful opportunity for dialogue around each affirmation's theme.

I hope you enjoy reading with your children as much as I have with mine!

Forever grateful to my grounded earth sign son & intense water sign daughter who inspire me everyday

Check out @theastrologymama on Tik Tok

This Book Belongs to

PICSES, CANCER, AND SCORPIO ARE THE THREE WATER SIGNS.

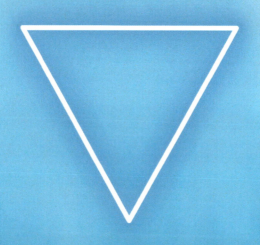

WHAT IS YOUR SIGN?

IF YOUR BIRTHDAY IS BETWEEN FEBRUARY 19- MARCH 20

YOU ARE A PICSES

IF YOUR BIRTHDAY IS BETWEEN JUNE 22- JULY 21

YOU ARE A CANCER

IF YOUR BIRTHDAY IS BETWEEN OCTOBER 23- NOVEMBER 21

YOU ARE A SCORPIO

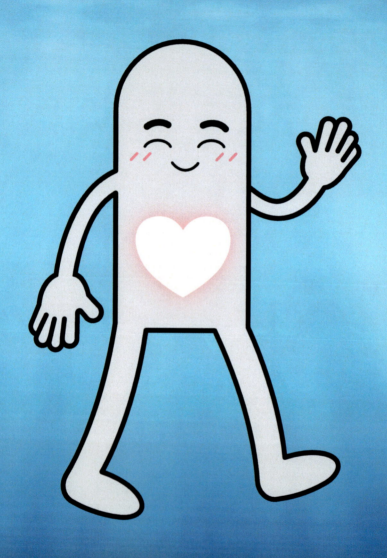

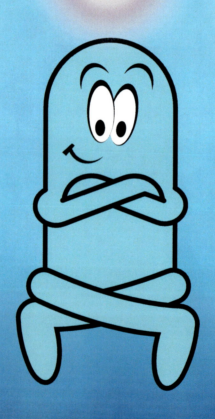

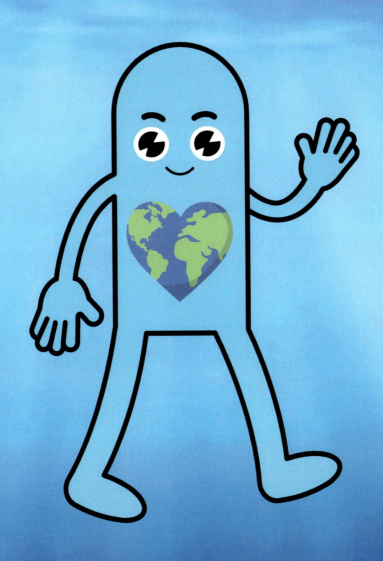

I AM GENEROUS

I AM IMAGINATIVE

I AM ALL OF THESE THINGS & SO MUCH MORE!

THE END.